Faith Walk

Girl Talk

JAMIE WATKINS

Paperback ISBN: 979-8-9945739-1-4
Hardcover: 979-8-9945739-0-7

Published & Cover Design By
My Peace of Happy
www.mypeaceofhappy.com

All scriptures are from the English Standard Version Bible

This book is dedicated to You.
The woman who desires to grow…
on her faith walk with God.

Hey Sis,
This book was written with you in mind… right where you are, not where you think you should be.

Faith isn't always neat. And real life isn't always pretty.
So, let's talk about it.

Some days your faith feels unshakeable. You believe boldly. You pray confidently. You trust that God is working every detail together for your good. And then there are days when life feels heavy — when your emotions speak louder than your hope, when prayers feel quiet, when you love God deeply… but you're tired, discouraged, uncertain, or still healing.

This book is for you.

For the woman who believes but still has questions.
Who prays but sometimes feels worn down. Who loves God yet is still navigating life, relationships, emotions, confidence, calling, and the constant balancing act of becoming who God created her to be.

This is Faith Walk Girl Talk.
In these pages, we'll talk about what faith really looks like in real life — when becoming feels both holy and human at the same time.

Girl talk.

God is faithful, even in the places you feel fragile. This is not a theology textbook. It's a heart-to-heart conversation.

You and me.

I'll ask you some questions along the way, and I've added journal pages so you can pause, reflect, and respond. Imagine us, cozy on the couch. I have my latte in hand, you have your favorite drink…

A safe space where our faith meets real life. A reminder that you are seen, deeply loved, covered by grace, and fully held by a God who knew every step of your faith walk before you ever took it.

So take a breath.

Bring your honesty, your tears, your questions, and your hope.

Let's walk and talk this out… together.

Your Sister in the Faith,
Jamie

A FIRM FOUNDATION

Before we start talking about healing, purpose, prayer, community or growth, we need a place to stand.

Every faith walk begins somewhere.
Mine began here…

Not with answers.
Not with clarity.
But with faith.
Faith in Jesus Christ.

Faith that doesn't require you to see the whole picture —
only to trust the One who holds it.

"But what does it say? 'The word is near you, in your mouth and in your heart' (that is, the word of faith that we proclaim); because, if you confess with your mouth that Jesus is Lord and believe in your heart that God raised him from the dead, you will be saved."
— *ROMANS 10:8–9*

This is where your faith walk begins…

PART ONE

A Foundation Rooted in Faith

Establishing Faith, Grace, Trust, and
God-Given Identity.

1

FAITH IS YOUR ANCHOR

Learning to Walk by Faith, Not by Sight

Faith is what anchors your peace, and it's where your walk continues…

It is a confidence that you live out; a settled position for and in things hoped for.

And I don't mean hope like the world uses it, "I hope this works out." I mean, "God, I trust You for it."

Even when you don't feel or see it, you trust that God is who He says He is. And He will do what He said He will do. Faith is the evidence before there *is* any evidence. It is when nothing about your situation says it will be okay, yet you walk in the full assurance that it will be.

Faith is not something we conjure up on our own, it's a God-assigned expectation that He has already gone before us and worked out what we just haven't seen yet.

What are you hoping for?

GIRL TALK

I've had seasons where my life felt like it was spinning out of control, and my emotions were running faster than my faith. Seasons where "peace" sounded like a good concept, but it wasn't my reality. Where my stressors were speaking louder than Scripture. I loved God, but my life was too burdened and weighed down to feel or see Him at work.

It was in those earlier, heavy seasons in my life that my faith was activated. I knew to pray, even if it was just to whisper…"God, I don't even know what to pray for. But I need You."

And Sis, let me tell you… that's enough. God will meet you right there.

Not in a whole sermon.
Not in a whole chapter of the Bible.
Not in a long prayer that flows perfectly.
Just in a whisper.

You know why? Because faith isn't about performance. Faith is about presence. It's about our heart posture.

God doesn't need us to be perfect; He just needs us to be connected. God has assigned each of us a measure of faith. Your measure of faith is the starting point for God's unseen work in your life and it's personal.

God assigned you a measure, enough to start, enough to grow, enough to believe Him in every season of your life. It is tailored to fit *YOU*, your calling, your capacity, your journey.

It's not something you can earn or qualify for. It's freely given to you because He loves you. Faith is your anchor when your emotions drift and attempt to betray you. It's the light when your clarity gets cloudy. It is what keeps you from believing the lies of your "inner me." Faith reassurances you when your hormones are out of whack, your moods are unpredictable and you feel like your brain can't be trusted. Your seasons will shift, BUT…

God doesn't.
God is a constant.
God is unchanging.
God is Faithful.

Faith doesn't always fix the moment. But it holds you down *in* the moment.
And every time you return to God, with the faith you have, even if it's just a whisper, you are anchoring your soul in the One who never changes.

I started doing puzzles over the past five years, and I love to use them as a reference. Faith is putting the picture together one piece at a time. Some pieces are more challenging to fit into the picture than others, but eventually it all comes together. Some of us get 500 pieces, while others get 5000 pieces. Either way, when you work with the pieces you've been assigned, you can be assured you'll get to the picture on the box.
You may be thinking that was a cheesy reference, but you get the picture, pun intended!

"Enough Faith for This Season"

There are seasons when God calls you to believe for things that don't match your current reality. You're praying, preparing, doing what you know to do, but nothing around you looks like it's aligning.

I want you to remember… God already gave you the faith you need for this moment. Wherever you find yourself right now, I want to encourage you to believe that you have enough faith to walk through this season, win this battle, pursue this calling or wait well in this holding space. You may not see it now, but keep believing.

Your measure of faith may not look like mine, but it is shaped for *your* faith walk. God will never call you to trust in what He hasn't already equipped you to believe for.

So today, instead of asking for "more faith," focus on using the faith you already have. That is where your peace grows and your confidence rises. Also, faith is not only believing and trusting God, but it's putting that faith into action!

Supporting Scriptures:

"Now faith is the assurance of things hoped for, the conviction of things not seen."
— HEBREWS 11:1

"And without faith it is impossible to please him, for whoever would draw near to God must believe that he exists and that he rewards those who seek him.
— HEBREWS 11:6

"So also faith by itself, if it does not have works, is dead."
— JAMES 2:17

PRAYER

"HELP ME TRUST THE MEASURE YOU GAVE ME"

Dear Heavenly Father,
Thank You for the measure of faith You've given to me.

Help me trust what You gave me.
Help me use what You placed in me.
Help me walk boldly and to live my faith out loud,
even when I cannot see the full picture.

God, strengthen me to believe Your promises over my
feelings. Posture my heart in Your peace, and anchor my
hope in Your faithfulness. Teach me to move, prepare and
show up with full confidence, not because I see the outcome
but because I trust that You hold it.

In Jesus's **Righteous** Name,
Amen.

LET'S TALK ABOUT IT...
What vision has God given you?

*Sis, let's grow better together to build your
Faith Walk with God.*

2

AMAZING GRACE
Receiving What Only God Can Give

Just like faith anchors you… Grace carries you.

Now this is the part where if I could sing "Amazing Grace," I would… but I can't, so I'll spare you. Besides, I'm sure you know the opening lyrics and can sing them on your own:

"Amazing grace! How sweet the sound,
that saved a wretch like me!
I once was lost, but now I'm found;
was blind, but now I see!"

We sing about God's amazing grace, and many believers can be found declaring, "It was nothing but the grace of God that brought me through." *But* sometimes, I wonder if we truly grasp just how amazing and undeserved God's grace really is!

God doesn't wait for us to "get it together," become worthy or impress Him with our accomplishments. God steps towards us *while* we are STILL wretched, STILL blind, STILL trying to fix ourselves and clean up our mess.

Maybe you're planning or actively trying to get yourself together before living for Christ.

How's that working out for you?

Let me guess… it isn't. No judgment here, truly.

My assurance comes from a familiar truth: I too thought I could clean up my act, then present myself to God. My efforts were futile, and like mine, yours will be too. Because grace is God doing for us what we can never do for ourselves. If we could fix ourselves, we wouldn't need His amazing grace.

When you truly see His amazing grace for what it is… everything changes!

Grace is God's love in motion toward us. Not because we deserve it. Not because we've earned it. Not because we prayed long enough, behaved well enough or "got it all together."

Grace is simply God being God, and God being good… because He is, in fact, good all the time.

GIRL TALK

There have been times in my life when shame rested on my shoulders like a worn, dirty cloth, and I felt completely undone. At my worst, I was an adulteress. And I wondered if I'd disappointed God beyond repair, even though I *knew* what His Word said.

It was grace that stepped into the gap between who I was and who God knew I was becoming. He knew the plans He had for me. Grace reminded me that God saw all of me, every season and STILL said, "I love her."

It was grace that rescued me.

All of my "I knew better" moments, the ones only hindsight made clear. The days when I felt, and sometimes was, anything but holy. Grace stepped into those too.

Not after I cleaned everything up.
Not after I made better choices.
Not after I felt worthy again.
Grace showed up in the middle of my mess.

Grace meets you where you are…
and walks forward with you.

That's the gift. That's God's Love. That is Amazing Grace!

It's not a one-time gift either. It's God continually pouring it over you, layer upon layer.

There will no doubt be growing pains, but grace is like a warm hug from God saying…
"Daughter, you don't have to be perfect. Here's my grace — receive it."

Now I feel the need to make something clear: Grace is not

permission to stay stuck. It's not God overlooking sin or pretending your pain isn't real. It is certainly not God lowering His standard.

Grace is power.
Power to grow.
Power to heal.
Power to become more aligned with God's heart.

Grace is God empowering you to rise to the life He designed you for.

"There Is Grace For You"

There will be days when you don't get it right. Days when you react instead of respond. Days when your emotions are loud and your faith feels small. Days when you think, *God surely must be tired of me by now.*

I want you to pause right there.

Remember grace is already present.
Grace is calling you to draw near.
Exhale.
Let God hold all of it with you.

Notice I said *with you,* because grace isn't always God taking it away from you or holding it for you. Sometimes, it's God giving you the grace to carry it.

Grace was built with our weakness in mind. And where we feel the weakest, that's when God's power shines the brightest.

Fight the urge to turn grace away. God's got an unlimited supply.

Don't be so hard on yourself…
Receive grace.
Walk in grace.
Extend grace… especially to yourself.

Supporting Scriptures:

"Let us then with confidence draw near to the throne of grace, that we may receive mercy and find grace to help in time of need."
— HEBREWS 4:16

"But God demonstrates His love toward us, in that, while we were STILL sinners, Christ died for us."
— ROMANS 5:8

"For sin will have no dominion over you, since you are not under law but under grace."
— ROMANS 6:14

"For from his fullness we have all received, grace upon grace."
— JOHN 1:16

"But he said to me, 'My grace is sufficient for you, for my power is made perfect in weakness.' Therefore I will boast all the more gladly of my weaknesses, so that the power of Christ may rest upon me."
— 2 CORINTHIANS 12:9

PRAYER

"LORD, TEACH ME TO RECEIVE YOUR GRACE"

Dear Heavenly Father,

Thank You for Your amazing grace. Thank You that I don't have to earn it, perform for it or qualify to receive it. Help me release shame, guilt and self-judgment and rest in the truth that Your grace is enough for me.

When I fall short, remind me that You are still near. When I feel unworthy, surround my heart with Your love. Teach me to walk in grace for myself and for others. And let my life reflect gratitude for the unearned, unending grace You so freely give to me.

In Jesus's **Matchless** Name,

Amen.

LET'S TALK ABOUT IT...
What part of your story still needs grace?

Who might God be asking you to extend grace to?

*Rest in knowing God's grace is sustaining your
present and redeeming your future.*

3

TRUST GOD ENOUGH

Leaning on Him When the Way Isn't Clear

You can't really *trust* God until you believe in His character and grace.

Trust is what steadies your steps.

If faith anchors you and grace carries you, trust is what keeps you moving forward when the path isn't clear. Just like faith, trust is active. It's choosing God *again and again,* especially when emotions rise, answers are delayed and life doesn't look like the prayer requests you've been petitioning God for.

Trust says:
"I don't see it yet… but I still believe God is working."
"I don't understand this… but I still know God is good."
"I don't like this season… but I still surrender my will to Yours."

Trust is the bridge between **what you believe** and **how you live**. It isn't denial. It's **direction.**

Trust keeps pointing you back toward God when uncertainty tries to pull you away.

When you truly trust God, you stop demanding full explanations and begin resting in His **promises** because His promises are rooted in His character.

God isn't asking you to understand everything, only to trust Him through anything.

This kind of trust brings freedom. A lifting of the weight you were never meant to carry. Letting go doesn't mean giving up; it means believing God's way is better than yours, and His plans are already covered.

GIRL TALK

The truth is… Trust can feel more like **trust falling**.
You cross your arms.
You squeeze your eyes shut.
And you fall backward, praying God is there to catch you.

Trust can feel scary. Nobody wants to hit the ground!

There were seasons when I trusted my plan more than God's. Times when waiting felt like punishment. Times when unanswered prayers looked like rejection instead of redirection. Times when I replayed every "what if" and worried myself into exhaustion.

Ulcers.
Anxiety.
Compulsive planning.
Sticky notes everywhere.

Plan after plan.
Always trying to control what was coming.

Trust falling.

Sometimes your biggest battle isn't against fear or the risk. It's against the urge to manage outcomes God never intended you to. Trusting God doesn't mean you never feel afraid. It means you keep walking with Him even when you do.

And yes. I did hit the ground by leaning on my own understanding and trying to do things my own way. You know what God whispered to my heart?

"Daughter… You don't have to control what I already covered."

Whew! In that moment, I realized I was slowly depleting myself trying to be my own safety net… while God had already gone ahead of me.

This is where trust deepens…
I'm reminded: There is no risk with God, only promises.

God is always present.
God will always catch me.
God will never fail.

Trust sounds like… "God, I don't know how… but I know You."

And that's enough. It's my God guarantee!

Now, I'm not trusting what I know — I'm trusting *Who* I know. **Are you trust falling… or simply *trusting*?**

Trust isn't about having all the answers. It's about trusting the One who does. It's loosening your grip on the outcome and tightening your hold on God's hand. And the more you lean into who He is, the less you feel the need to control everything you can't.

"Trusting God Anyway"

There will be seasons when God calls you to walk forward with unanswered questions.

Seasons when obedience feels costly.
Seasons when your heart wrestles between surrender and self-reliance.

That's when trust becomes sacred work. It's not about being comfortable or certain. Trust is built in the late-night tears you cry while still choosing to pray.

It is built in the conversations you have with God when you're disappointed but still showing up. Trust is built when you unclench your fists and whisper, "Okay, God… Have Your way."

You can stop trying to map the path.
Instead, you can hold God's hand.

And as you do, His promises begin to quiet your fear.
Peace replaces panic.
Purpose replaces pressure.
And your confidence shifts from what you can control… to the One who controls it all.

Peace doesn't come from clarity.
Peace comes from trust.

And trust grows when you remember God's promises:
- He is faithful
- He is present
- He is working
- He is good

Write it. Speak it. Pray it. Hold on to it.

Let it ground you when doubt tries to creep in. Because trust isn't something you master once. Trust is something **you practice daily**.

Supporting Scriptures:

"Trust in the Lord with all your heart, and do not lean on your own understanding."
— Proverbs 3:5

"When I am afraid, I put my trust in you."
— Psalm 56:3

"It is the Lord who goes before you. He will be with you; he will not leave you or forsake you. Do not fear or be dismayed."
— Deuteronomy 31:8

"You keep him in perfect peace whose mind is stayed on You, because he trusts in You."
— Isaiah 26:3

"Commit your way to the Lord; trust in him, and he will act."
— Psalm 37:5

"And blessed is she who believed that there would be a fulfillment of what was spoken to her from the Lord."
— Luke 1:45

"For all the promises of God find their Yes in him. That is why it is through him that we utter our Amen to God for his glory."
— 2 Corinthians 1:20

PRAYER

"LORD, TEACH ME TO TRUST YOU"

Dear Heavenly Father,
Thank You for always being faithful, even when I struggle to
fully trust you. You see every hidden worry, every silent fear,
every place where my heart still
tries to hold control.

Help me trust Your heart when I cannot see Your hand.
Remind me that You see what I cannot and that
Your plans for me are good.

Lord, when I start to lean on my own understanding, gently
guide me back to You.

Help me to rest when impatience rises.
Steer me to Your promises when fear whispers lies.
Slow me down and steady my soul when I try to run ahead
of You.

Teach me to release control.
Teach me to walk by faith and not sight.
Teach me to trust You fully and completely.

Quiet the noise inside me so I can hear Your voice. Help me
remember that I am never falling;
I am always being held.

I choose to believe You are working…
Even here.
Even now.
Even when I don't understand.

In Jesus's **Mighty** Name,
Amen.

LET'S TALK ABOUT IT...
Where is God inviting you to trust Him more deeply?

What promise about God's character brings peace to your heart?

You don't have to trust perfectly.
You just have to trust God enough.

4

WHO GOD SAYS YOU ARE

Standing Firm in Truth Over Feelings

Who are you, really? When the titles fade, the roles shift and the pressure lifts?

I'll tell you…
You are God's daughter.
You are loved.
You are forgiven.
You are redeemed.

Do you know that you were God's daughter before you were anything to anyone else?

Your identity is a big deal to God, and therefore it should be a big deal to you. God lovingly created you with intention. He shaped you with purpose. He called you, chose you and set you apart.

When your worth and purpose are rooted in God, it redefines who the world says you are. It may even redefine who **you've believed you are**.

Sis, God never asked you to *become* worthy.

He declared that you already are.

GIRL TALK

My identity is something I struggled with for a very long time. If you read my memoir, *My Peace of Happy*, then you already know this about me.

I lived most of my life trying to be who I thought everyone wanted me to be. As a result, I became a perfectionist, a performer, a people-pleaser. I defined my worth by other people's opinion of me. I adjusted my personality to make others comfortable. I shrunk to fit into places that were never designed for me, and I dimmed my light because other people said it was too bright.

If you had asked me back then who I was, I would've told you…
I am a daughter.
I am a sister.
I am an aunt.
I am a friend.
I am an employee.
I am a wife.
I am a mother.

I knew who I was to everyone else… but I didn't really know who I was **to myself or to God.**

So, let me ask you…

Who are you when no one needs you to be something for them?

It wasn't until I started to understand who I was to God that I began shaking off opinions I'd allowed to define me. Opinions that said I wasn't good enough. I was too hard to love. I talked too much. I laughed too loud. Even the ones that praised me for being "strong" and "together." I refined identities I'd taken on based on my trauma…

All of those opinions carried weight…
Those identities added pressure,
either the pressure to be
or the pressure not to be.
And both were crushing.

It was during my self-love journey, rediscovering myself through God's truth, that I finally learned this:

Identity is not something you *achieve*.
Identity is something you *receive*.

Because when you surrender your life to Jesus Christ, you don't become who the world expects — you become who God already says you are.

God declares you are…
A new creation.
Worthy.
Purposed.
His masterpiece.
A royal priesthood.
A temple for the Holy Spirit.

"Becoming Who God Says You Are"

There will come a moment in your faith walk when God gently asks you to lay down every false identity you've worn. The strong one, the quiet one, the fixer, the good girl, the guarded one, the one who always holds it together.

Not because those roles never mattered, but because **they were never meant to define you.**

True identity flows from one truth:
You belong to God, and He calls you His daughter.

And here's another beautiful truth…

You don't have to fight for belonging when you already belong. You don't have to hustle for acceptance when **you are already accepted.**

You don't have to audition for love when you're already loved.

Your identity isn't rooted in who you are to others.
It's rooted in who you are **to God.**

Don't ever doubt who you are in Christ or how much God loves you!

God declares, **"I have called you by name. You are mine."**

Supporting Scriptures:

"For we are his workmanship, created in Christ Jesus for good works, which God prepared beforehand, that we should walk in them."
— Ephesians 2:10

"But you are a chosen race, a royal priesthood, a holy nation, a people for His own possession, that you may proclaim the excellencies of Him who called you out of darkness into His marvelous light."
— 1 Peter 2:9

"Therefore, if anyone is in Christ, the new creation has come: The old has gone, the new is here!"
— 2 Corinthians 5:17

"But now thus says the Lord, he who created you, O Jacob, he who formed you, O Israel: 'Fear not, for I have redeemed you; I have called you by name, you are mine.'"
— Isaiah 43:1

PRAYER

"LORD, REMIND ME WHO I AM"

Dear Heavenly Father,
Thank You that my identity is safe in You. Thank You that I am not defined by my past, my titles, my roles, my mistakes or the opinions of others but by Your truth and Your love.

When I forget who I am, remind me that
I am Your daughter.

When insecurities surface, anchor me in Your Word.
When comparison creeps in, refocus my heart on You.
When I am tempted to shrink, remind me I was created to stand out.

Lord, remove every false label I've carried, spoken by others or whispered in my own mind. Heal the parts of me that believed I wasn't enough… and the parts that believed I had to be everything.

I belong to You.
And that is enough.

In Jesus's **Excellent** Name,
Amen.

What labels have been placed on you that God never wrote?

LET'S TALK ABOUT IT...

What steps can you take to walk out who God says you are?

PART TWO

Becoming Who God Called You to Be

Growing into Wholeness, Surrender, Purpose, and Strength.

You are fully known, fully loved and fully His.

5

BECOMING WHOLE

Letting God Heal What's Been Broken

Wholeness doesn't equal perfection.

Wholeness isn't pretending you're fine.

And it doesn't mean suppressing your story so you look "strong."

Wholeness is living loved, fully, freely and rooted in God.

In order for you to walk in and live out who God says you are, you need to allow Him into the rooms of your heart you've closed off. I know this may stir up a bit of fear or anxiety at the thought of it…

Remember **you trust God enough**. Besides, there is nothing about you that He doesn't already know.

The places layered with disappointment, fear, shame, control, comparison, silent grief or even secret sins you avoid confessing… all of this will eventually cripple your Faith Walk. The unhealed places will quietly whisper lies about who you are and who God is until you finally surrender them to Him.

The world teaches you to "push through."
But God invites you to **heal through.**
Sis, you can only walk fully in who you are when you allow
God to tend to the wounds that once told you who you weren't.

It's God's desire to make us whole.

Wholeness doesn't mean nothing ever broke you. It means…

What broke you no longer defines you.
Your story no longer owns you.
Your worth is no longer negotiated by people.
Your identity is secure, not fragile.

God doesn't expect us to "tough it out."
God doesn't rush our healing. He meets us inside of it.
And sometimes the most spiritual thing we can do is **tell the truth about what still hurts.**

He can only heal what we're willing to bring to Him.

Forgiveness is your key to wholeness.
Grace says God forgives you.
But then wholeness requires action on our part.

Are you starting to see a pattern? It's a relationship: God does His part, we do ours.

Sometimes the hardest act of forgiveness isn't for *other people…*
it's for **yourself**.

For the choices you regret.
For the red flags you ignored.
For the version of you who didn't know what you know now.

Shame will keep you stuck in pieces, but forgiveness allows healing to bring them together.

Some of us believe God forgives *everyone else* more easily than He forgives us. We confess, but we keep punishing ourselves. We say we're forgiven, but we still live condemned.

God is clear that He is faithful and just to forgive us.

Wholeness happens when you stop arguing with God about what He has already forgiven — and, unlike us, forgotten.

What about when your wholeness means extending forgiveness to others? I know… this is where it gets tender.

Stay with me.

Forgiveness is not pretending it didn't hurt.
It's not excusing what was wrong.
And it doesn't mean instant trust or reconciliation.
Forgiveness is releasing your heart from carrying what God never meant for you to hold.

Not because *they* deserve it, but because *you* **deserve peace**.
You don't heal by holding on. You heal by letting go and letting God lead you into freedom.

It takes courage to stop pretending.
When you finally do, God can start restoring.

I hid behind my smile for so long, I started to believe my own
facade. I told myself I was staying positive. I was being strong.
I was "keeping the faith." But my body was telling the truth:

I was losing weight.
Losing sleep.
Losing my joy.
On the outside, I looked like I was living.
Inside, my spirit was silently grieving.

And the hardest truth?
I wasn't just lying to myself…
I was lying *to God* and about God.

Every time the Holy Spirit nudged me to cry out…
To fall at the altar…
To run to His Word…
And I said, "No, I'm good."
I denied God access to my heart.

I wasn't good.
I was tired, burnt out and overwhelmed. I excused myself
out of healing. I told myself there were people going through
"far worse," and God needed to tend to them instead. But the
whole time, God was whispering:
"Come to Me… and I will give you rest."

He was waiting for me to cast my cares on Him.
He was waiting for me to surrender my will in exchange for His.
He was waiting to heal my broken heart.

My healing to wholeness was not a comfortable journey, but it was necessary…

I started to notice the patterns I hid behind.
I realized the strength I praised was sometimes emotional survival.

I recognized where I overperformed because I felt unseen.
I saw where I poured out for everyone else but never felt full myself.

I discovered a version of myself behind the mask, who desperately needed me to forgive her. And let God love her.

Step by step, healing happened.
Tender.
Layered.
Grace-filled.

I share this with you so you realize your faith walk will sometimes be uncomfortable, but also so you know it will *always* be worth it.

God will never shame you for needing healing.
You don't have to be whole to come to God.
You become whole by walking with Him.
And Sis, there's something else…

I'll hold your hand as I say it…
gently, honestly and with love.

When forgiveness is avoided, healing is often delayed.

Not because God is withholding healing…
but because unforgiveness keeps reopening the wound.

Unforgiveness has a way of disguising itself.
It can look like strength.
Like boundaries.
Like "I'm over it."

But beneath the surface, it keeps your heart tense, guarded and braced for impact. Over time, what isn't healed begins to bleed into your relationships, your body, your peace and even your faith.

God doesn't expose unforgiveness to punish you…
He reveals it so He can heal you.
Never rushed. Never forced.

God is patient.
But He loves you too much to let you stay stuck.
That's the God we serve.

Unfortunately, you may have been hurt; you may still wear some scars. But your pain isn't meant to be permanent. Allow yourself permission to trust the loving hands of the One who can help you become whole.

"The God Who Heals Softly"

There are wounds that time didn't fix.
But God never forgot about them.

He won't rush you.
He won't scold you.
He is waiting until your heart feels safe enough to unwrap
them with Him.
He is your safe space.

Healing with God looks like…
Him sitting with you in the memories.
Him wiping the tears you cry alone.
He speaks truth where lies may live.

And slowly, the sting fades.
The memories soften.
You rest in His perfect peace.

Supporting Scriptures:

"He heals the brokenhearted and binds up their wounds."
— Psalm 147:3

"He restores my soul. He leads me in paths of righteousness for his name's sake."
— Psalm 23:3

"There is therefore now no condemnation for those who are in Christ Jesus."
— Romans 8:1

"Come to me, all who labor and are heavy laden, and I will give you rest."
— Matthew 11:28

"The Lord is near to the brokenhearted and saves the crushed in spirit."
— Psalm 34:18

"If we confess our sins, He is faithful and just to forgive us and cleanse us from all unrighteousness."
— 1 John 1:9

"Cast all your anxiety on Him, because He cares for you."
—1 Peter 5:7

PRAYER

"LORD, MAKE ME WHOLE IN YOU"

Dear Heavenly Father,
Thank You for seeing every unseen bruise on my heart and loving me through every piece of my story. I give You the parts of me I've hidden, protected, avoided or ignored. Heal the places I still carry silently. Restore the parts of me that forgot what peace feels like.

Teach me to release survival mode.
Teach me to stop shrinking.
Teach me to receive love without fear.
Teach me to become whole, not in my own strength but in You.

When the healing feels slow, remind me that You are patient with me. I trust that my life is becoming whole by filling it with You.

Help me forgive where it still hurts.
Help me release what no longer serves my healing.
Help me to receive the forgiveness You have already given me.

In Jesus's **Powerful** Name,
Amen.

LET'S TALK ABOUT IT...
What will becoming whole look like for you?

Know that healing prepares the heart for surrender. Surrender positions you for purpose. Lean in.

6

SURRENDER YOUR YES
Releasing Control and Choosing Trust

If you think the journey to wholeness is hard, surrendering your yes can feel even harder. And most people won't tell you that. Somewhere along the way, this idea crept into the body of Christ that if you are "saved enough," nothing should feel difficult. That if you truly love God, you won't struggle.

That simply isn't true.

Even Jesus wrestled with surrendering His will.
Not wanting to be separated from the Father, He prayed…

He went back and prayed again and yet again, a third time, so intensely that His sweat fell like drops of blood.

That tells me that in His humanity, the weight of surrender was heavy. Yet He still chose to submit to the Father's will over His own.

It should come as no surprise then that surrendering our yes, in our humanity, is going to feel hard sometimes too. Surrender isn't a process to complete; it's consistently choosing

God's way over your own. A faithful rhythm of releasing control. Surrendering your yes to God is an act of obedience.

It is saying…
Yes to whatever God has for you.
Yes to His will.
Yes to His Word and aligning your life with it.

It won't always be easy.
And while it may stretch you, great is its reward.

GIRL TALK

There were times when I said "yes" to God, but my heart still wrestled behind the scenes. It sounded like…

"Yes, God… but can You please do it my way?"
"Yes, God… but I'd like to approve the outcome first."
"Yes, God… but only if the timing is convenient."

Have you ever been there?
Maybe you're there now.

I wanted the blessing of surrender without the discomfort of releasing control. I was a major control freak! I trusted God, but I still clung to my plans. I still tried to hold the pen and write the story myself. And when things didn't go how I expected, frustration, disappointment and doubt showed up.

But here's what God gently showed me:
Obedience isn't obedience…

if you only agree when it feels easy.
And surrender isn't surrender
if you're still trying to manage the outcome.

Ouch! That realization humbled me. And painfully so. I can be transparent and say if God hadn't allowed it to hurt out of love, I don't know that I would have learned to let go. Some lessons I had to learn the hard way.

Now God had me right where we wanted me…
Not perfect, but **willing**.

To trust that His ways really are higher.
And Sis, the more I surrendered my yes, the lighter I became…

Control is heavy.
Fear is heavy.
Pleasing people is heavy.
Being a "fixer" is heavy.

It took a lot of grief, a bankruptcy and a divorce, but finally, I got it.

Once I surrendered my plans, my will and my ways to God, He was able to have His way in my life…

And nothing surrendered is ever wasted.
Your job is the yes.
God's job is the rest.

It isn't about control.
It isn't God trying to restrict you or limit your life.
It isn't Him demanding perfection or waiting for you to "get it right."

Surrendering and obedience is an invitation to live aligned with God's heart, to trust His wisdom over your own, to walk closely enough with Him that His voice becomes familiar.

Now this will not be easy. Especially when you've survived by being strong, capable, independent and a control freak like me.

When you've had to figure things out on your own for so long, releasing control can feel scary, even unsafe.

Surrender sounds like:
I don't have to know what's going to happen.
I don't have to hold everything together.
I don't have to play God in my own life.
I just have to follow the One who already sees the end from the beginning.

True obedience flows from trust, not fear.

It is response, not obligation.
It is love in action, which leads to alignment.
Because we know God first loves us, we love Him.

And here's a hard truth:
Sometimes obedience will cost you something.

It may cost you comfort.

It may cost you approval.

It may cost you your pride, your timelines or the version of life you imagined.

But what God gives in exchange is always greater.

Peace.

Clarity.

Purpose.

Freedom.

Alignment.

Wholeness.

And most importantly, closeness with Him.

There will be moments where obedience feels inconvenient or unfair. Moments where surrender feels like loss. Moments where trusting God stretches you in ways you didn't expect. But on the other side of surrender, there is always fruit.

God's asking you to follow Him step by step.

You don't lose yourself in surrender — you finally become who you were created to be.

"The Yes That Changes Everything"

Surrender is not about losing your life; it's about handing your life back to the One who gave it to you. When you surrender your yes to God, you're agreeing to follow Jesus wherever He leads.

Jesus didn't just talk about obedience.
He lived it. It's because of His yes we now have life.

When the path feels uncertain, as it often will,
Your yes says…

God, I trust You more than I trust me.
God, I believe Your way leads to life.
God, I'm willing, even when it's hard.

And the beautiful part:
Every yes surrendered to God becomes a seed of purpose. He uses your obedience to shape you, stretch you and align your heart with His. You may not always understand the assignment, the season or the stretching, but you can always trust the Good Shepherd.

The life you are saying yes to is not a life of pressure. It is a life of **presence, purpose and becoming like Jesus.**
Sis, your surrendered yes is powerful.

Obedience positions you for purpose.
And surrender prepares your heart to carry it.

Supporting Scriptures:

"Saying, 'Father, if you are willing, remove this cup from me. Nevertheless, not my will, but yours, be done.'"
— LUKE 22:42

"If anyone would come after Me, let him deny himself and take up his cross daily and follow Me."
— LUKE 9:22

"No discipline seems pleasant at the time, but painful. Later on, however, it produces a harvest of righteousness and peace for those who have been trained by it."
— HEBREWS 12:11

"For my thoughts are not your thoughts, neither are your ways my ways, declares the Lord."
— ISAIAH 55:8

"For my yoke is easy, and my burden is light."
— MATTHEW 11:30

Jesus said, "If you love Me, keep My commandments."
— JOHN 14:15

PRAYER

"LORD, I SURRENDER MY YES TO YOU"

Dear Heavenly Father,
Thank You for loving me enough to lead me. Thank You for
Your Word, Your guidance and the example Jesus gave of
what it means to surrender fully to Your will.

Today, I surrender my yes to You.
Yes to Your will.
Yes to Your Word.
Yes to the life You call me to live.

Help me to obey Your commands not out of fear but out
of love because You first loved me. When my flesh wants
comfort more than calling, strengthen me. When my feelings
rise louder than my faith, steady me. When I want to lean on
my own understanding, gently draw me back to trust in You.

Teach me to deny myself daily, take up my cross and follow
Jesus with a willing heart and surrendered spirit.

Lord, align the desires of my heart with Your plan and will
for my life. And remind me that obedience always leads me
closer to You.

I surrender my plans, my comfort and my control, believing

that Your way is always best.
Here I am, Lord. My answer is yes.

In Jesus's **Holy** Name,
Amen.

____

____

____

____

____

____

____

____

____

____

____

____

____

____

How does your life reflect your "yes" to God?

*Your yes may not come easy, but I do hope
that it is peaceful.*

<h1 style="text-align:center">7</h1>

PURPOSE ON PURPOSE

Living Intentionally in Your God-Given Assignment

Purpose is God-designed. Divine. Intentional. Personal. It's the thread that weaves your story together, your faith, your grace, your trust, your identity, your wholeness and your surrender… all aligning to something exceedingly and abundantly greater than you could ever imagine on your own.

Purpose is not accidental. It isn't something you earn through effort or achievement. Your purpose was authored by God before the foundations of the world. You were created to **walk in it**, not stumble upon it.

When you walk faithfully in your calling.
When you surrender your yes to God's will.
When you live authentically as the woman He created you to be.

Purpose is who you are in alignment with God's plan for you. It's how you serve others with the resources He's entrusted to you. So lean into your gifts, your story and even your broken places.

GIRL TALK

I used to think my purpose was wrapped up in roles… being a

wife, a mother, a friend, a helper, serving others from the places I'd stepped into. And while there is purpose in those roles, I remember asking God more than once, "Is this it? Is this all I'm really meant to do?"

It turns out…
My *roles* didn't define my purpose.
My *journey* revealed it.

It was the hard lessons that shaped me.
The big mistakes that humbled me.
The long waiting that prepared me.
The painful trials that pruned me.
And God who purposed me through it all.

There was a time I thought my past disqualified me.
I thought if people really knew…
What I survived,
What I endured,
What I walked through,

They wouldn't listen to me.
They wouldn't respect me.
They wouldn't see God in me.

I wouldn't have guessed that the depression, the toxic marriage and even the divorce would become the doorway through which He would call me into ministry to empower women through mental wellness, well-being and purpose.

But what I learned is this:

The very things I wanted to hide were the exact places God wanted to speak through.

When I stopped pretending…
When I stopped minimizing…
When I stopped acting like I'd always been strong…

God started using my story to reach women who needed proof that healing was real.

What I once saw as breaking, God was using as building. What I thought would disqualify me, God used to equip me.

God's purpose is never wasted, even when the path feels confusing. Purpose is a journey, not a destination.

I genuinely can't wait to see what else God has in store for me today, tomorrow (God-willing) and every day after that. God's purpose shows up in the little things, the big things and everything in between.

Purpose isn't always glamorous. Sometimes it looks like quiet faithfulness, showing up in your home, at work, in your relationships or in your community with love and integrity. Sometimes it looks like everyday acts of obedience no one else ever sees.

And yes, sometimes it looks like walking through hard seasons with faith, grace and trust, believing that your story, just like I pray mine is doing for you now, is being shaped for someone else's healing as well as your own.

This is something I'm very passionate about because purpose isn't just lived, it's shared. **Your story matters.**

Not the polished version.
Not the edited-for-comfort version.
Not the "I've always been strong" version.
The real one.

When God brings you through something, it's never just for you. Your testimony becomes a tool in God's hands.
Your survival becomes someone else's hope.

Your healing becomes evidence that transformation is possible. There is power in what God has done in your life.

And when we hide our stories, minimize them or pretend we've never "been there," we limit how God can use us to reach others.

Purpose on purpose means stewarding your story well.
It means showing up authentically, without shame, without pretending, without spiritual filters that make it seem like faith erased your humanity.
God doesn't just use the *arrival*.
He uses the *process*.

When you refuse to be vulnerable, you may think you're

protecting yourself or even protecting God's reputation.
But the opposite is true.

When you act like you've never struggled…
Never doubted…
Never fallen…

You unintentionally communicate that God only works with "together" people.

And that does a disservice to the very people who are standing where God once met you.

When you pretend you've never been there:
- You minimize the power of God to deliver.
- You silence hope for those still in the middle.
- You turn purpose into performance.

But God is not glorified by perfection.
He is glorified by **transformation**.

Your story is proof that God still heals, still restores, still redeems, still calls, still uses imperfect people for holy purposes.

Oh, and let me point out: Sharing your story doesn't always mean sharing everything with everyone.

Wisdom matters. Boundaries matter. Timing matters.
But silence out of shame is not humility, it's bondage.

Purpose requires honesty.
When God invites you to share, it's not to expose you — it's to free someone else.

Paul didn't hide his past.
David didn't clean up his story.
Mary Magdalene wasn't ashamed of where she came from.

The woman at the well ran back and told everyone what Jesus did for her. And because she did… lives were changed.

**Your testimony doesn't disqualify you.
It authenticates you.**

Sis, don't rob someone else of hope because you're uncomfortable being honest. Allow God to repurpose your pain.

"Living Your Purpose, on Purpose"

Living your purpose, on purpose, requires intentionality.

Purpose grows when you step out in faith. When you use the gifts God has given you, even imperfectly. When you show up honestly. When you love well. When you steward not only your talents but your story.

God needs you to be present. He needs your willingness. He needs your yes, even when it feels vulnerable.

Purpose is living a life of faith, grace, trust, identity, wholeness and surrender. And every day, your life quietly becomes a light for someone else who is still finding their way.

Your story matters. Your calling matters. Your life is not random, it is divinely intentional.

Supporting Scriptures:

"'For I know the plans I have for you,' declares the Lord, 'plans for welfare and not for evil, to give you a future and a hope.'"
— Jeremiah 29:11

"And we know that in all things God works for the good of those who love Him, who have been called according to His purpose."
— Romans 8:28

"Many are the plans in the mind of a man, but it is the purpose of the Lord that will stand."
— Proverbs 19:21

"And they have conquered him by the blood of the Lamb and by the word of their testimony, for they loved not their lives even unto death."
— Revelation 12:11

"Let the redeemed of the Lord say so, whom He has redeemed from trouble."
— Psalm 107:2

"Commit your works to the Lord, and your plans will be established."
— Proverbs 16:3

PRAYER

"LORD, HELP ME WALK IN MY PURPOSE"

Dear Heavenly Father,
Thank You for creating me with intention and calling me according to Your divine purpose. Help me see the unique design You placed within me and give me the courage to live it out fully, faithfully and honestly.

Your purpose for me *is* my purpose.

Teach me to discern Your voice over the noise of the world. Help me say yes to the call You have for me, even when it's uncomfortable, uncertain or requires vulnerability. Remind me that You are working all things together for my good and the good of those around me.

Give me courage to walk in my gifts, to steward my story well and to love and serve with humility. Let my life be a love letter to you that points others toward You.

Help me trust that where You lead, You will also equip.

Teach me to live my purpose, on purpose.

In Jesus's **Exalted** Name,
Amen.

____

____

____

____

____

____

____

____

____

____

____

____

____

____

____

Who needs hope from the very place you've survived?

____

____

____

____

____

____

____

____

____

____

____

____

____

____

____

Walk boldly in the purpose God designed for you.

8

FULLY EQUIPPED

Growing in All You Need for Life and Godliness

Sis, you already have what you need.

And no, you don't need a million dollars (though if you have it, that's great!).

Through Christ, you already have everything required to live this life and walk out your purpose, your calling, your divine assignment. However you choose to describe the plans God had in mind *before He even formed you in your mother's womb…* you are equipped for them!

I tell women all the time:
"You are enough. You are equipped. You are empowered with purpose."

But I also know it's not enough for *me* to say it if *you* still feel like you're lacking…
or behind…
or missing something everyone else seems to have.

Have you ever felt that way?
Because I have.

GIRL TALK

To this day, I am still my biggest critic. But the more I grow in my faith walk and stay close to God through prayer and His Word, the more I appreciate who He created me to be. And I know this for a fact:

God makes no mistakes.

Yet I still have days when I think…
Lord… are You sure You picked the right girl?

I recognize my gifts.
I see God at work in and through me.
And still, sometimes it feels like I'm standing outside myself,
watching someone else do the things God has called me to
do.

But here's a thought:
Maybe that's exactly how it's supposed to be.
Because when you live surrendered…
it's not really you — it's God in you.

Realizing this has given me so much relief…
less anxiety…
and the freedom to simply *be*.

The truth is, on my own, I am not enough.
But God begins where I end.
His strength fills the gaps.
His power equips where I cannot.

And through Him, I am fully equipped. **And so are you.**
As believers, we have Jesus Christ Himself and His gift of salvation. God has also gifted us His Holy Spirit.

With those gifts alone, we're empowered. Often, we are waiting to feel ready, to *want* to do the "thing".

It's okay if you don't feel ready. Chances are, you won't.
This is where surrender and obedience step in…

Moses didn't feel ready.
Gideon didn't feel qualified.
Esther didn't feel prepared.
Jeremiah didn't feel capable.

And still, God called them.
Equipped them.
Used them anyway.

Ready or not, here God calls!

But God doesn't call you into purpose and then walk away.
We have a helper, the Holy Spirit.

You are not walking this journey alone.

He walks with you.
He leads you.
He carries you when needed.
He equips you every step of the way.

Let me also say this: Feeling unqualified isn't a sign that your faith is weak.

It simply means you are aware that you need God.
That is the best place to be.
Totally reliant and depending on God.

Your goal should never be confidence in yourself, but full confidence in God.

Because He's God.

Sometimes the equipping looks like:
- Healing old wounds
- Confronting limiting beliefs
- Learning healthy boundaries
- Releasing unhealthy patterns
- Growing spiritually and emotionally
- Trusting God in unfamiliar territory

God's got you though all of it.

Your faith walk will stretch you.
You will still have days when you cry.
You might still question God.
You may still feel vulnerable or unsure.

Just remember you are not doing it on your own.

"Fully Equipped for My Purpose"

You don't have to become someone else to live out your calling. God has already placed inside you what you need to walk faithfully with Him. He will bring out the best He's placed in you! Through Christ, you are fully supplied.

That means you don't have to wait…
God equips you as you go.

You may think, *If only I had more confidence, more resources, more clarity… then I could really step into my purpose.*

But God didn't misjudge your capacity.
He didn't overestimate your strength.
And He didn't underestimate what He placed inside you.

So today, instead of asking, "Am I enough?"
try asking: "God, how would You like me to use what You've already given me?"

You *are* equipped.
You *are* empowered.
And you *are* purposed.
Take a moment to breathe that in.

Supporting Scriptures:

"His divine power has granted to us all things that pertain to life and godliness, through the knowledge of Him who called us to his own glory and excellence."
— 2 Peter 1:3

"Before I formed you in the womb I knew you, and before you were born I consecrated you; I appointed you a prophet to the nations."
— Jeremiah 1:5

"Not that we are sufficient in ourselves to claim anything as coming from us, but our sufficiency is from God."
— 2 Corinthians 3:5

"But the Helper, the Holy Spirit, whom the Father will send in my name, He will teach you all things and bring to your remembrance all that I have said to you."
— John 14:26

"I can do all things through Him who strengthens me."
— Philippians 4:13

PRAYER

"LORD, HELP ME BELIEVE I AM ENOUGH"

Dear Heavenly Father,
Thank You for reminding me that through You, I already
have everything I need for life and godliness. Help me release
the pressure to perform, to compete or to compare myself
with others before I feel worthy
of Your calling.

Teach me to trust Your strength more than my own feelings.
Because it is in my weakness that Your strength is made
perfect.

When doubt speaks, let Your truth speak louder. When fear
rises up, remind me that You go before me, beside me and
are within me.

I surrender the parts of me that still question if I'm enough,
and I receive the truth that **in You, I already am.**

In Jesus's **Beautiful** Name,
Amen.

Who can you serve with the gifts God has equipped you with?

Living a
God-Centered Life

A Rhythm of Intimacy, Scripture,
Community, and Identity Expressed.

*Move forward confidently, courageously
and faithfully.*

9

SPEND TIME WITH GOD
Creating Sacred Space for Intimacy

You cannot grow close to someone you never spend time with.
This includes God.

Prayer is not an item to check off your list.
It's not a last resort when all else fails.
It's a conversation that builds relationship.

Prayer is communicating with God.
Prayer is connecting with God.
Prayer is building intimacy with God.

And what about praise and worship?

They are how love is expressed in your relationship with God.
It is what we were created to do.

Prayer draws you close.
Praise lifts your eyes.
Worship recenters your heart.

God wants quality time with *you*.

Intimacy with God grows the same way intimacy grows in any relationship: through **consistency, vulnerability and presence.**

When you talk to God, listen for Him, sit quietly with Him and open His Word, your faith becomes lived, not just learned. You'll begin to recognize His voice in the gentle nudges, the still moments and even the uncomfortable stretching seasons.

This allows your heart to rest in God.
It's where He meets you with love, wisdom, correction, comfort and direction.

Prayer will sometimes look like deep worship.
Other times, it looks like crying in your car.
Another time, it looks like silence… because you don't have the words. **God receives it all.**

When you pray, you aren't just talking to God — **you are being shaped by Him.**

And when you praise and worship Him, even before things change, your heart remembers who God is.

God's presence helps shape your well-being.
It helps you to realign your priorities.
It softens your heart.
Heals what's been broken.

In His presence, you learn to love yourself better because you start to see yourself through God's eyes. Shame loses its voice.

Fear loosens its grip. Peace becomes familiar.

Your view of God grows from God… to Father… to Daddy
… to Friend.

God is everything you need Him to be.

Prayer doesn't always change your circumstances
immediately…
but praise and worship will always change **your posture**.

And that inner transformation?
That's where intimacy with God lives.

GIRL TALK

I think you know by now that I'm going to keep it real with
you. My prayer life wasn't always what it is now. I remember
hearing pastors quote 1 Thessalonians 5:17, "Pray without
ceasing," and thinking, *Well, that's unrealistic. Who has time
to pray all day long?*

Now?

I feel like I'm praying all the time… and I sort of am.

Prayer has become natural. Beautiful. A lifestyle.

Sometimes I'm asking the Holy Spirit for wisdom, to help me
with a decision. Or just to give me the right words to say.

Sometimes it's peace to help me sleep when I awake with anxious thoughts.

A lot of times, I'm petitioning God on behalf of myself and others. Fervently pleading for comfort for the bereaved, or interceding for those who have lost their way.

Other times, I'm listing off everything I'm grateful for. Or worshiping God in the middle of my situation before anything changes.

I think my favorite times are when I'm silent…
Waiting for God to speak. Listening for Him to whisper to my heart. Expecting Him to reassure me that He is near.

I talk to God out loud. In my spirit. While driving. While working out. At 3 a.m., like when He downloaded the vision and title for this book. I enjoy consulting the Holy Spirit and chatting it up with Jesus!

That's *now*… for the most part.
But there are other times, even still when…
I fall asleep. My mind wanders to my to-do list.
I start scrolling social media and don't even remember picking up my phone.

"My bad, God." (Even that is a prayer.)

It's like that sometimes. Don't overthink it.
Prayer and worship can feel intimidating if you think you have

to "sound super spiritual," or pray for hours, or only say all the right things. But think about how you talk to someone you love. It's honest. It's real. It's not always polished. That's what God wants. Your heart, not rehearsed prayers.

Some seasons, your prayer may simply be…
"Help me, Lord."
"Thank You, Jesus."
"Sorry, God."

That's still prayer.
That still counts.
And God listens.

Sometimes I imagine God smiling and saying,
"I'm just glad you're here."

Your presence matters in His presence.

So, how do you grow your intimacy with God and develop a lifestyle of worship? I'm glad you asked!

Simple, Yet Significant:
How to Build Intimacy with God
Time with God doesn't have to be formal to be holy.

1. Create Space for God
Not rigid, but intentional.
- Morning quiet time
- Prayer walks

- Talking to God while driving
- Sitting in silence
- Playing worship music

2. Pray Honestly and Pray Scripture

Tell God the truth, the raw version. He already knows, and He deeply cares. When you don't have the words, borrow His. His Word doesn't return void.

3. Praise Before You See Results

Praise is your weapon. It shifts your focus and leaves a mark… reminding your heart who God is, even when circumstances haven't caught up yet.

4. Listen, Don't Just Talk

Prayer includes listening for His peace, His prompting, His still, small voice. Remember prayer is a two-way conversation. Listen for the wisdom and direction of God.

5. Worship and Surrender

Worship isn't just singing, it's yielding your heart and saying, "God, You're worthy, right here." Love on God, for who He is, not what He's done or you want Him to do, but just because He's an awesome God!

6. Invite God Into Everything

Work. Motherhood. Business. Marriage. Friendships. Healing. Dreams. Grief. Success. Failures. Etc.

God wants all of you, not just your "church moments."

"Spending Time With God"

Prayer is the space where we quiet the noise of the world and lean into the heart of our God who knows us best. It's where our worries soften, our defenses fall and our soul gets to breathe.

When you intentionally make space for God, you begin to notice His nearness in ways you may have missed before, in the peace that settles your spirit, in the clarity that comes when you pause.

As your intimacy deepens, God gently reminds you:
You are seen. You are loved. You are His.

Let prayer be more than words.
Let praise be more than music.
Let worship be the posture of your heart.

Supporting Scriptures:

"Call to Me and I will answer you, and will tell you great and hidden things that you have not known."
— JEREMIAH 33:3

"And this is the confidence that we have toward Him, that if we ask anything according to His will He hears us.
— 1 JOHN 5:14

"You make known to me the path of life; in Your presence there is fullness of joy; at Your right hand are pleasures forevermore."
— PSALM 16:11

"God is spirit, and those who worship Him must worship in spirit and truth."
— JOHN 4:24

"Praise Him for his mighty deeds; praise Him according to His excellent greatness!
— PSALM 150:2

"I will bless the Lord at all times; His praise shall continually be in my mouth."
— PSALM 34:1

PRAYER

"LORD, DRAW ME CLOSER"

Dear Heavenly Father,
Thank You for inviting me into Your presence. Thank You
that I don't have to earn my way to You, I simply need to
come. Teach me to slow down, to quiet my mind and to
make room in my life to sit with You.

Help me to crave Your presence more than keeping busy,
welcoming distraction or seeking approval.

Remind me that building intimacy with You isn't a task, it's a
gift…
That I GET to talk with You.
I GET to praise You.
I GET to worship You.

When I don't have the words, reassure me that You already
know my heart and You meet me right
where I am.

Help every moment I spend with You to transform how I
live, love and walk out my faith.

In Jesus's **Precious** Name,
Amen.

LET'S TALK ABOUT IT...
What are the strengths and weaknesses in your relationship with God?

How do you intend to grow your intimacy with God?

May your days be marked by closeness with God, and your life shaped by prayer, praise and worship.

10

YOUR DAILY BREAD

Nourishing Your Spirit Through God's Word

Just like your body needs food daily to live, your spirit needs the Word of God. You can't fully live for God without engaging with His Word.

God's Word is nourishment to our souls.

It strengthens you.
Anchors you.
Corrects you.
Comforts you.
Reminds you who you are and who God is.

The Bible is God speaking, His heart, His character, His promises, His truth, His guidance.

All God breathed for you so you can walk through this life fully equipped and spiritually alive.

When we spend time in the Word, we're connecting with God and renewing our mind. The Word of God is what helps us to weather any storm.

Feelings change.
Circumstances shift.
Heaviness lifts.
And God's Word restores.

GIRL TALK

I didn't *always* love reading the Bible. I don't know too many
Christians that can say they have and not be lying. There were
times I didn't understand it, times it felt condemning and times
I said to myself, "I read my Bible on Sunday in church. That's
good enough."

Maybe you've felt that way too.

Sometimes it felt easier to listen to a sermon, read a devotional
or scroll through inspirational quotes than to open my Bible
and sit with God.

But the more I grew in my faith, the more I realized…
Secondhand faith is not the same as firsthand relationship.

Don't get me wrong — sermons can help give context and
practical application, which we need.
But your pastor shouldn't be your only source for the Word of
God. Books help you too. I'm trusting God this one will serve
you well.
But this won't always speak to your exact circumstance.

Podcasts help (very popular these days).
But nothing replaces you and God, together, in His Word.

So, where am I now?
The Word feels alive to me.
Comforting.
Convicting sometimes.
Strengthening.
Even soothing at times.

It's like God sits beside me while I read and whispers, "This is for you."

Do you ever feel like that? Like God is talking directly to you? Well, He is.

How awesome is that!

I love that I can read the same scriptures over and over, and depending on what season I'm in or what I'm going through at the moment… God speaks to me differently.
Yet it is always exactly what I need.

Just like with prayer, it doesn't always look perfect. I will dare to say there *is* no perfect!

So, what does daily Word time actually look like?
Some days it's reading deeply and journaling.
Some days it's meditating on one verse.
Some days you miss it altogether…
And you pick it back up the next day.
And every time you show up, you grow closer and deeper.

"Your Daily Bread"

The Word of God feeds your soul… slowly, daily, consistently.
You may not always feel something dramatic, but God's Word
is doing a work within you.

The Word reshapes your thinking and softens your heart.
It strengthens your faith and deepens your trust.
It makes you whole.

You no longer have to ride the roller coaster of emotions, be
tossed about by your triggers or blinded by your traumas. You
get to walk in faith and live by a definitive truth in the Word
of God.

Let God's Word become your daily bread, not just something
you read but something you live.

Supporting Scriptures:

"But he answered, 'It is written, Man shall not live by bread alone but by every word that comes from the mouth of God.'"
— MATTHEW 4:4

"All Scripture is breathed out by God and profitable for teaching, for reproof, for correction and for training in righteousness."
— 2 TIMOTHY 3:16

"Do not be conformed to this world, but be transformed by the renewal of your mind, that by testing you may discern what is the will of God, what is good and acceptable and perfect."
— ROMANS 12:2

"Heaven and earth will pass away, but my words will not pass away."
— MATTHEW 24:35

"The grass withers, the flower fades, but the word of our God will stand forever."
— ISAIAH 40:8

PRAYER

"LORD, MAKE YOUR WORD ALIVE IN ME"

Dear Heavenly Father,

Thank You for the gift of Your Word, steady, faithful and true. Help me to hunger for it and understand it. Help me to see what You want to show me about You, about myself and about the life You've called me to live.

Let Scripture take root in my heart.
Let the wisdom of Your Word guide my decisions.
Let Your truth shape my thoughts and strengthen my faith.

When I feel distracted, discouraged or distant, gently draw me back to Your truth. And as I read, help me not only gain knowledge but experience transformation and true sanctification so my life reflects Your Word in how I live, love and walk with You.

In Jesus's **Eternal** Name,
Amen.

LET'S TALK ABOUT IT...
What impact has the Word of God had on your life?

How can you better prioritize the Word of God in your life?

____

____

____

____

____

____

____

____

____

____

____

____

____

____

____

Nourish your soul, renew your mind and guide your steps in the Word of God everyday.

11

WE GROW BETTER TOGETHER
Finding Strength in Community and Connection

Our faith walk was never meant to be a solo journey.

Yes, your relationship with God is personal…
but it was never designed to be isolated.

From the very beginning, God established community as part of His divine order.
We are formed, strengthened, corrected, encouraged and sustained through relationship.

We can love God deeply and still struggle if we try to walk this faith walk alone.

You can pray, read the Word, worship and still feel weary when you're disconnected from the people God placed around you.
Because growth happens best in **community**.

God uses people.
He speaks through people.
He heals through people.
He sharpens us through people.

Staying connected in the Body of Christ is not a suggestion, it's a necessity.

You are one part of a greater whole. And when one part is disconnected, the entire body feels it.

Community reminds us who we are when we forget. Accountability keeps us steady when we're tempted to drift. Godly relationships help us grow where isolation would keep us stuck.

You know my motto, "We grow better together!"

GIRL TALK
As much as I love the idea of community…
I don't always like people.
Shocking, right? But here's why I say that.

Because people can disappoint you.
People can misunderstand you.
And yes… people can hurt you.

It only takes a few church wounds, broken relationships or seasons of betrayal before it starts to feel safer to say,

"God and I are good. I don't need anyone else."

And so I get it. I really do.
But here's what I've learned, and you guessed it… the hard way! It's that:

Healing doesn't happen in hiding.
And faith doesn't mature in isolation.

Some of the greatest growth in my life didn't happen in prayer alone, it happened in **conversation**. In having someone I could open up to. Confide in. Someone who could see me, not judge me and still walk with me.

It happened in **accountability**.
In being lovingly challenged.
In having someone say, *"Sis, I love you… but what you're doing is not it!"*

Iron sharpening iron isn't always comfortable.
Sometimes sparks fly.
Sometimes pressure is applied.
But sharpening produces strength.

Isolation dulls us.
Community refines us.

So, while I may not always *like* people… I've learned to *love* people.

Why?

Because God loves people.
People matter to Him.
And what matters to God must matter to me.

By design, we need each other. And by command, we are called to love one another.

And here's something else I've come to realize:
You can't fully heal what you refuse to let others see.

God often uses **safe, trusted people** to bring clarity when we're confused, correction when we're off track and confirmation when we're unsure.

God designed our faith walk to be walked out **together**.
Community is about participation.
Because growth happens better… together.

Here's Why Community Matters in Your Faith Walk:

- **Community provides accountability**
  Someone who loves you enough to ask hard questions.
- **Community offers perspective**
  When emotions cloud your judgment.
- **Community brings encouragement**
  When your faith feels low.
- **Community creates covering**
  When you're tired of being strong.
- **Community reminds you that you belong**
  And belonging matters.

"We Grow Better Together"

From the very beginning, God called people into relationship with Him and with one another. Community isn't an optional add-on in this Christian life; it's essential.

Ever feel stuck, like you've hit a wall and stopped growing? That's often because growth requires connection. Not just surface-level interaction, but meaningful, God-centered relationships where you can be known, supported, encouraged and lovingly challenged.

Community is where faith is practiced out loud. God often uses people to answer prayers you've been praying privately. He uses conversations to confirm what He's already whispered to your heart. He uses trusted relationships to strengthen areas that would otherwise remain fragile.

And yes, community can be messy. People aren't perfect. But walking this faith walk alone carries its own risk. When you walk alone too long, it's easier to believe lies, carry burdens you weren't meant to hold and drift from the support God lovingly placed around you.

You don't need everyone.
You may not need many.
But you do need **someone**.

God grows us through people. And when we stay connected, we don't just survive — **we thrive**.

Supporting Scriptures:

"Iron sharpens iron, and one man sharpens another."
— Proverbs 27:17

'For just as the body is one and has many members, and all the members of the body, though many, are one body, so it is with Christ."
— 1 Corinthians 12:12

"Two are better than one because they have a good reward for their toil. For if they fall, one will lift up his fellow. But woe to him who is alone when he falls and has not another to lift him up!"
— Ecclesiastes 4:9–10

"And he said to him, 'You shall love the Lord your God with all your heart and with all your soul and with all your mind. This is the great and first commandment. And a second is like it: You shall love your neighbor as yourself.'"
— Matthew 22:37–39

"Let us consider how to stir up one another to love and good works, not neglecting to meet together."
— Hebrews 10:24–25

PRAYER

"LORD, CONNECT ME AS YOU INTEND"

Dear Heavenly Father,
Thank You for being my constant companion, and for the gift
of community You place around me to strengthen, support
and sharpen my faith.

Lord, heal any places in my heart that have been wounded
by relationships, betrayal or disappointment. Help me not to
close myself off in self-protection but to trust You enough to
remain open to the connections You are calling me into.

Give me discernment to recognize healthy, life-giving
relationships you've assigned to me. Lead me to people who
love You, who walk in truth and who will encourage me to
grow. Teach me how to be a good friend, a safe space and a
source of encouragement to others as well.

Help me release fear of being seen and replace it with faith
in Your design. Let me grow in accountability, humility and
love as I walk alongside others who are pursuing You. Thank
You for reminding me that we are better together!

In Jesus's **Marvelous** Name,
Amen.

LET'S TALK ABOUT IT...
What role does your community play in your life right now?

____

____

____

____

____

____

____

____

____

____

____

____

____

____

____

Connect to relationships that sharpen your faith, guard your heart and encourage your growth.

12

WHO YOU REPRESENT
Living Out Your Identity as God's Daughter

As rewarding as it is, I'll be the first to tell you that this faith walk can be challenging work.

It's also **holy work, necessary work and heart work.** It's not always easy… but be encouraged, it does become easier.

As you continue to anchor yourself in your faith, embrace His grace, trust Him and lean into your wholeness and who God says you are, you are becoming more like Him.

While you're being intentional about maturing your faith through prayer, praise, worship and the Word…
While growing better together in the body of Christ…
You are deepening your relationship with God.

And the process of transformation and sanctification?
It's not just for you, it ties back to community.

You are salt and light.
You are walking evidence of who your Father is.
No, you won't ever be perfect.

But be intentional and allow God to tend to your heart so that what grows from your life looks like Him.

You not only represent Him.
You *re-present* Him.

Your faith is visible.
Your fruit is formed.
Your life speaks without saying a word.

GIRL TALK

If you were around in the 1990s, you probably remember the WWJD (What Would Jesus Do?) bracelets. You may have even had one. I actually wear one now… not the bright, multi-colored nylon kind from back then but a subtle sterling silver Morse code version. It serves as a way to hold myself accountable.

Have you ever done or said something, and someone asked, "Aren't you supposed to be a Christian?"

Or maybe, at some point, you've said it yourself.
That's not judgment. That's feedback.

We don't have to announce that we're a believer.
Our fruit will speak for us.
And when we miss it?
It's an invitation to realign, repent and return.

Because yes, I *am* supposed to be a Christian.
A daughter of the King.

A follower of Christ.

How I live my life matters.
I don't get to do whatever I want.
I can't say whatever I feel like.

There are moments when my flesh wants to respond faster than my faith. When patience feels optional. When kindness feels inconvenient. When peace feels far away.

This chapter isn't about pressure, it's about awareness.

Like me, you're human. You wake up in this flesh every day and have to choose to die to it. Pick up your cross. Follow Jesus.

When we pause before we react or choose grace when offense is easier, we reflect the nature of Christ.

Sometimes representation looks like biting your tongue.
Other times, it looks like saying sorry first.
Or choosing growth over being right.

When I pray, I ask the Holy Spirit to help me stay kingdom-minded. To align my thoughts, words and actions with Who He is.

Scripture reminds us to guard our hearts because everything flows from it…

When your heart is led by God, your life reflects God. That's where the fruit of the Spirit becomes evident, not just for show but as evidence of a surrendered life.

The fruit of the Spirit is something that grows when you stay connected to the Source. Love, joy, peace, patience, kindness, goodness, faithfulness, gentleness and self-control are byproducts of a life rooted in Christ.

Being kingdom-minded doesn't mean you ignore real life, it means you filter life through God's perspective. You choose to think about what honors God and serves your well-being.

What we allow into our mind will eventually show up in our lives,
so being mindful to renew your mind and guard your heart is critical.

People may never read their Bible, but they will read your life. So, let it reflect Who you belong to.

**Here's How to Live as a Daughter of the King
(Without Pressure)**

1. Begin with Awareness, Not Self-Criticism
Representation starts with noticing, not judging.
Ask yourself:
- What fruit is showing up in my life right now?
- Where might God be inviting growth?

This isn't about shame. It's about **connection**.

2. Guard Your Heart Before You Guard Your Image

What you allow in will eventually come out.

Be intentional about:

- Conversations you entertain with others
- Thoughts you rehearse in your head
- Spaces that stir up unrest in your spirit

A guarded heart produces grounded responses.

3. Pause Before You React

Representation often looks like restraint.

When emotions rise, practice the pause:

- Breathe
- Pray
- Choose response over reaction

Remember: Sometimes honoring God looks like *not saying anything at all.*

4. Let the Fruit Speak for You

You don't need to explain your faith. Let it be seen.

Ask yourself:

- Does my response show love?
- Does my tone carry peace?
- Does my face reflect gentleness?
- Does my behavior point back to God?

Fruit grows when you remain rooted, not when you try harder.

Stay connected.

5. Realign Quickly When You Miss It

You will miss it sometimes. That doesn't disqualify you.

When you do:

- Own it
- Apologize if needed
- Return to God

Repentance is not punishment, it is restoration.

6. End Each Day with a Kingdom Check-In

Ask gently:

- Where did I reflect God well today?
- Where can I grow better tomorrow?

Then, release the day. Growth happens over time.

"Fruit That Represents"

Living as a representative of the Kingdom means your life points back to the Father, genuinely, purposefully and consistently.

When you respond with gentleness instead of defensiveness.
When you walk in self-control instead of reaction.
That's fruit.

You don't grow fruit by trying harder.
You grow fruit by staying rooted.

God isn't asking you to fix everything at once. He's inviting you to stay connected and let Him do His work in and throughout your life. He will prune what doesn't serve you and strengthen what does.

Let them know Him by your fruit.

Supporting Scriptures:

"But the fruit of the Spirit is love, joy, peace, patience, kindness, goodness, faithfulness, gentleness, self-control; against such things there is no law."
— GALATIANS 5:22–23

"In the same way, let your light shine before others, so that they may see your good works and give glory to your Father who is in heaven."
— MATTHEW 5:16

"Keep your heart with all vigilance, for from it flow the springs of life."
— PROVERBS 4:23

"Finally, brothers, whatever is true, whatever is honorable, whatever is just, whatever is pure, whatever is lovely, whatever is commendable, if there is any excellence, if there is anything worthy of praise, think about these things."
— PHILIPPIANS 4:8

"I am the vine; you are the branches. Whoever abides in me and I in him, he it is that bears much fruit, for apart from me you can do nothing."
— JOHN 15:5

PRAYER

"ALIGN MY HEART AND MIND"

Father God,
Thank You for trusting me to represent You.
Help me live with awareness, not pressure. Teach me to
guard my heart and renew my mind with intention.

When my flesh wants to lead, remind me to pause and
choose Your way.

Holy Spirit, cultivate Your fruit in my life. Shape my
reactions, help me to "fix my face," soften my responses and
align my thoughts with heaven's truth. Help me reflect Your
love, patience and peace in every
space I enter.

Let my life point back to You, not for attention
but for Your glory.

In Jesus's **Wonderful** Name,
Amen.

LET'S TALK ABOUT IT...
How does your fruit represent—and re-present—Jesus?

LET'S TALK ABOUT IT...

What personal areas do you need God to help you cultivate?

Keep your heart tender, your mind anchored and every season fruitful.

Hey, Sis,

I pray this conversation has blessed you as much as it has blessed me.

This isn't the book I thought I was going to write.
It's the book God gave me — with you in mind.

I'm so honored He trusted me to share this space with you. These pages were written prayerfully and intentionally, with the hope that you'd feel seen, encouraged, and reminded of who you are in Him.

This may be the end of the book, but it's only the beginning of what God is doing in your life. I'm excited about what He's ignited — or maybe even reignited — in your spirit, and the plans He still has unfolding for you.

If you didn't take time to reflect, journal, or respond to the questions along the way, go back and do that. Let this book continue to speak to you in new seasons and new places of becoming.

And keep it close. Return to it when you need steadying, when you need reminding of His promises, and when you need to remember who He says you are.

May these pages serve you well on your faith walk — or simply as a trusted "friend" whenever you need a girl talk moment.

I'm rooting for you to become everything God purposed for you to be. And I'm praying He blows your mind along the way.

With Love,
Your Sister in the Faith,
Jamie

FREE DOWNLOAD

SCAN AND DOWNLOAD

ACKNOWLEDGMENTS, With Thanks!

To the women (too many to name) God placed along my faith walk… Thank you!

Thank you for walking with me when my faith was forming and when it was being tested. For praying when I didn't have the words. For reminding me of truth when I forgot it. For loving me through growth, through questions and through seasons when I didn't always get it right.

Thank you for your patience when I was learning.
For your grace when I stumbled.
For your honesty when I needed correction and your gentleness when I needed comfort.

Some of you strengthened my faith by your words.
Others by your example.
Some simply by staying.

You showed me what sisterhood in Christ looks like. You showed me what it means to sharpen one another, to bear one another's burdens and to point each other back to God when life feels heavy or confusing.

This book carries pieces of what I've learned by watching you live out your faith in real life, not perfectly but faithfully. Your obedience, your prayers, your encouragement and your love helped shape the woman I am and the faith walk I carry today.

May God honor what you've poured into me, and may He continue to grow us better together.

With Gratitude and Love,
Jamie

Special mention and a heartfelt thank you to my executive pastor, Brandon Sardik, and my father-in-love, Rev. Dr. Ricky Watkins, for their wisdom, theological guidance and support. Safeguarding the integrity of God's Word, its context, meaning and reflection of His character was essential to me, and their counsel was invaluable.

ABOUT THE AUTHOR

Jamie Watkins is a minister of the gospel, speaker, author and writing coach passionate about helping women embrace well-being, purpose and joy in every aspect of their lives.

Known for her authentic, faith-forward approach, Jamie creates spaces where women can grow spiritually without pressure or perfection. Her work blends biblical truth, emotional wellness and real-life conversation, encouraging women to deepen their relationship with God while navigating the realities of everyday life.

As the founder of *My Peace of Happy*, Jamie's mission is rooted in helping women experience peace from the inside out through faith, intentional living and personal growth. She speaks and writes with the heart of a sister, offering encouragement, clarity and practical wisdom for women who love God but are still becoming.

Jamie is the author of *My Peace of Happy* and *Faith Walk Girl Talk*, where she invites readers into honest conversations about faith, healing, purpose and community. Her writing reflects her belief that faith isn't about having it all together — it's about staying connected to God through every season.

When she's not writing or speaking, you can find Jamie enjoying life with her husband, cherishing family time with her children or spoiling her toy poodle, Reesie Cup.

OTHER WORKS BY JAMIE WATKINS

My Peace of Happy: A Self-Love Journey to Happiness, Purpose and Lifestyle Success

90 Day Lifestyle Success Journal: Empowering Self-Love, Happiness & Purpose

Empowering Me: A Self-Love Journal for Teen Girls

Plan with Purpose: A Guided Planner for Women

CONNECT WITH JAMIE

Stay encouraged and connected beyond these pages.

Website: www.mypeaceofhappy.com
Instagram: @mypeaceofhappy
Facebook: @mypeaceofhappy
YouTube: My Peace of Happy
Email: booking@mypeaceofhappy.com

www.ingramcontent.com/pod-product-compliance
Lightning Source LLC
Chambersburg PA
CBHW062145150726
47991CB00006B/2184